bedroom
essentials

ROS BYAM SHAW

bedroom
essentials

RYLAND
PETERS
& SMALL
London New York

Designer Emilie Ekström
Senior editor Henrietta Heald
Picture research Claire Hector and Emily Westlake
Production Deborah Wehner
Art director Gabriella Le Grazie
Publishing director Alison Starling

ISBN 1-84172-603-6

10 9 8 7 6 5 4 3 2 1

First published in the United Kingdom
in 2004 by Ryland Peters & Small
Kirkman House
12–14 Whitfield Street
London W1T 2RP
www.rylandpeters.com

Text copyright © Ros Byam Shaw 2004
Design and photographs copyright
© Ryland Peters & Small 2004

A CIP record for this book is available from the British Library.

Printed and bound in China.

contents

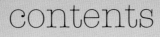

getting the

elements right

planning the space

Making a plan sounds dull – the sort of thing your Mum might nag you to do, or your teacher might tell you off for not doing. Most of us want quick results. However, as with so many tasks in life, groundwork pays off. Unless you live in a house with plenty of generously proportioned rooms, your bedroom will have to fulfil more than one role. As well as being somewhere to retreat for intimacy, privacy, rest and sleep, it will probably have to house clothes, shoes and bags. It may also be the only reliably quiet place in a busy family home and therefore the room where you choose to work.

Above The sleeping platform is a neat solution to separating a bedroom area in a one-room flat.
Left With meticulous planning and careful choice of furniture, working and sleeping spaces can be elegantly combined.
Opposite, left Storage and bed line two walls of this small bedroom. Books and toys are readily accessible on open shelves, while clothes and more toys are tucked away in cupboards. All in all, it is a recipe for that rare thing – a child's bedroom that is easy to keep tidy.
Opposite, right A curtained landing has been ingeniously utilized as impromptu guest accommodation.

- The most important piece of furniture is **the bed**. Decide on its size and style first. This is the **starting point** of your plan.

- **Fitted furniture** is almost always a more **efficient** use of space than unfitted.

- Fitted wardrobes can be designed to make **an alcove for the bed**. This is an effective way to ensure that a **wardrobe does not dominate** a room.

- Clothes will be the main **storage issue**. Measure roughly how much **hanging space** you need before acquiring a wardrobe. Be generous.

Left Both space-saving and ideal for games, bunk beds remain a perennial favourite with children.
Below The steeply sloping ceiling of a bedroom in the roof is charming, but the arrangement of furniture needs careful consideration in order to minimize bumps on the head.
Opposite Space is a glorious luxury, here emphasized by the expanse of polished wooden floor and the lack of curtains at the tall casement windows. The design of a large room needs just as much care as a small one, but perhaps not quite as much cunning.

Space is always an issue in a bedroom. Usually, the problem is lack of space: how to fit in enough storage around the bed and still leave sufficient elbow-room to get dressed without having to stand on it.

In a small room there may be only one obvious place to put the bed – but using every scrap of available wall, floor and underneath space takes a bit more thought and ingenuity. You don't necessarily need to get out the graph paper and tape measure, although it can help, but you do need to sit and think about what goes where before you buy a giant wardrobe or even a small bedside table; fitted wardrobes might result in a better use of space, and your bedside table might need to double as a desk.

Think about lighting and where you will need to have it. Think about where you would like the radiator (it is not usually difficult or particularly expensive to move a radiator). And don't forget the space that is taken up by wardrobe doors when they are open, or drawers when they are pulled out.

colour schemes

The traditional wisdom when choosing a colour scheme for a bedroom is to favour colours considered to be gentle, soothing and therefore sleep-inducing: pastels, creams, off-whites and neutrals. But colour is deeply subjective. While crisp, white linen certainly has the advantage of looking invitingly clean, there is no reason why the rest of the décor should follow suit. A bedroom is essentially a private space and, as such, can be the arena in which to express entirely personal taste.

Above Chaste white walls are strongly contrasted with the rich strawberry red of bed linen and the strong purple of the bedside shelf. The effect is simple and dramatic.
Left Pastels, traditionally thought the most suitable bedroom shades, are used here to elegant effect.
Opposite The snowy bed linen in this theatrical room looks whiter than white in contrast with the scarlet of the walls, the purple suede of the headboard, and the midnight-black background of the mural above.

It is difficult to prove, but nevertheless generally accepted, that colours can have a direct effect on emotions. However, the rules are far from universal. After all, who can say what the colour that you see as red looks like to anyone else? Of all rooms in the home, your bedroom should be the one where you feel most free to indulge in the red that warms your heart, the blue that makes you smile.

Another, less personal aspect of colour is its ability to create certain optical effects. Pale and receding colours from the blue and green side of the colour spectrum tend to make spaces expand, while warm, 'advancing' colours – ranging from red through orange to yellow – pull walls in around the observer.

For creating a sense of space and increasing light, you cannot beat that most popular and innocuous of non-colours, white. But an all-white scheme can be too dazzling and clinical for a room in which you want to feel safely cocooned.

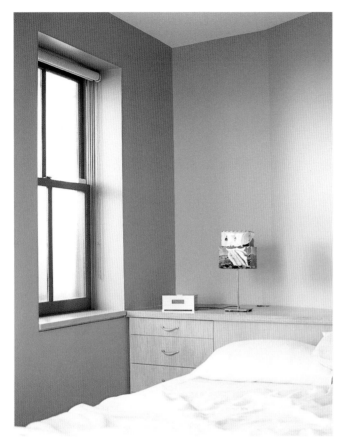

Instead, you can use white walls, or a more forgiving off-white, as the blank canvas on which to superimpose other favourite colours, whether you are making sharp contrasts with bright, strong shades or creating a subtler effect with paler, faded or neutral tones.

The advantage of a white, or near-white, background is that you can ring the changes when you tire of a particular colour scheme. You might even want to introduce a winter and summer palette – with darker, warmer curtains, bedspread, cushions and rugs to make you feel cosy on icy mornings replaced by gentle pastels for spring and summer.

In recent years the fashion has been for plain fabrics and wall treatments. This ought

Opposite, left Red is a rich, positive colour, especially a red that is closer to purple than orange. Pale pink diaphanous curtains tone well with this shade of red, and the soft textures of the cushions and wall hanging make the bed look inviting.
Opposite, above right A stripy quilt pulls together the colour scheme in this sophisticated bedroom.

Opposite, below right The honey-brown hue of natural wood brings warmth to a room with clean, contemporary lines.
Above A pale terracotta wall paint complements the golden tones of a headboard and integral drawers.
Right Different shades of blue give this room a dreamy quality, ideal for rest and relaxation.

to make dealing with colour more straightforward. In fact, if everything from the floor covering to the curtains is a single colour, particular care must be given to the balance between these different shades and to the way they interact with one another. The latter is more difficult to predict than you might imagine. Simply holding a piece of fabric against a paint chart never tells the whole story. In this situation, a useful tool is a colour board – a pinboard to which you can attach samples of fabric, carpet and paint to see how well they coexist. The larger the samples and expanses of paint, the more accurately you will be able to predict the finished effect.

Above A disciplined colour scheme gives a room a certain formality as well as a deep sense of calm. The very strong contrast in this room between the dark walls, headboard and pillow borders and the bright white paintwork and snowy bedspread is mitigated by the mid-tone of the natural wood floor.

Above right Neutral tones have a more relaxed feel because there is less play on contrast.

Right and opposite The effects of contrast are softened in this room, which draws from a palette of whites, off-whites and soft grey. Texture adds both visual and tactile interest to a study in monochrome.

• A **flourish of pattern** in a room dominated by plains can add **coherence** to a colour scheme – for example, **a faded chintz** that brings together the pale wood of the floorboards and the lilac of the walls, or **a multi-coloured stripe** that links more contrasting shades.

• Paint **a large piece of cardboard** with the shade of paint you are considering and prop it against **all the walls** of the room in turn. It won't look **quite the same** in one position as in another.

• Colours vary depending on **how they are lit**. A bedroom colour should look good in artificial and **natural light**.

Below Apart from the bed, storage is the most important element of the furnishings in any bedroom. Fitted wardrobes are an extremely efficient use of space and, as here, can combine sections for hanging and folding as well as that bedroom essential, a full-length mirror. There are many excellent modular ranges that can be purchased off the peg and put together to suit personal requirements, and these tend to be less expensive than commissioning bespoke joinery.

Above The style of bed you choose will be the key to the decoration of the room. Here the feel is robust and almost industrial: a metal bedstead, which uses poles and connectors reminiscent of scaffolding, sheltering under a metal spiral staircase, which may once have been a fire escape.
Opposite A completely plain low divan, dressed in white, evokes a mood of meditative simplicity – an effect reinforced by the restrained, almost monastic architecture of the room.

furniture & storage

Whether it is a modern divan or an antique extravaganza, the bed remains the central feature of any bedroom, and is likely to be the single most expensive item of furniture in the room. While a bed's appearance will set the style for the décor, its comfort is equally important. Choosing the right mattress is not simply a question of ensuring a good night's sleep; it can also prevent back problems. If you prefer a soft mattress, choose a bed with a sprung divan base. Mattresses suitable for laying on wooden slats tend to be much firmer. Whatever kind of mattress you invest in, remember to turn it a couple of times a year to keep the wear evenly spread.

Antique bedsteads can be irresistibly beautiful but apparently impractical, since they are rarely a standard size – Victorian double beds, for example, are often far too narrow to satisfy modern notions of king-sized comfort. However, a Victorian double bed can make a pleasantly generous 21st-century single and, even if you cannot find a duvet of exactly the right size, there are companies which will make a bespoke mattress to fit an old bed frame for a price that compares favourably with a good-quality standard mattress.

Second only in importance to the bed is storage. Most of us lack a separate dressing-room or a walk-in wardrobe, so somewhere to keep clothes fresh and dust-free must be found in the bedroom itself. Never before have so many people owned so many clothes. Where once a few hooks and a wooden chest would have sufficed, we now require ranks of drawers, tiers of shoe racks and metres of hanging rail.

Opposite, left Sleeping space in this warehouse conversion can be set up almost anywhere – all it takes is a couple of tatami mats, futons, pillows and a well-placed chair.

Left and below A stylish bedhead gives presence to an ordinary divan – and makes it more comfortable to sit up in bed. The plain upholstered bedhead (left) looks clean and contemporary, while the huge piece of roughly carved wood (below) seems to shelter the bed as well as giving the room character with its organic shape and beautiful grain.

Right and far right, top and middle Carefully laundered and folded bed linen offers an aesthetic pleasure.

Far right, bottom A bedside table should be big enough to hold books and a glass of water.

Freestanding wardrobes can be found in all shapes, sizes and styles – from the cheap-and-cheerful zip-up fabric module to the cedar-lined behemoth. Similarly, chests and chests-of-drawers can be anything from valuable antiques to painted MDF (medium-density fibreboard). Antique pieces are not necessarily more expensive than good-quality new furniture, but antique wardrobes that predate 1900 tend to be too narrow for modern coat-hangers. And don't buy an old wardrobe or chest that smells of mothballs – or your clothes will ever afterwards smell like great-grandmother's attic.

A large bedroom can accommodate freestanding wardrobes and chests, but in small rooms fitted cupboards will give you a lot more volume per square metre of floor space. Fitted cupboards can reach right up

to the ceiling and into corners and alcoves. You can install fitted cupboards along a whole wall, or design them to flank the bed with high cupboards across the top, making a recess into which the bedhead fits. Inevitably, this will mean that some cupboards are more easily accessible than others, and you will probably find that a certain amount of juggling is a biannual necessity – packing summer clothes into boxes banished to high cupboards in the winter and doing the same with bulky woollens in the summer.

Labelling boxes in which you keep things for infrequent use can save a lot of time and rummaging. A Polaroid photograph attached to the front of stacked boxes of shoes provides a neat form of quick identification.

Once you have somewhere to lay your head and hang your jacket additional furnishings are more a question of space and choice than necessity. At the top of the list should be a bedside table, providing an invaluable surface for a reading

Opposite, above left A wood-panelled bedroom is enriched by iconic pieces of 20th-century design: an undulating screen by Charles Eames and a leather upholstered chaise by Edward Wormley.

Opposite, above right An antique wooden chest, probably designed to hold documents, looks entirely at home in a modern bedroom, while its shallow drawers make ideal storage for socks, pants, ties and other small items of clothing.

Opposite, below Bespoke storage, like this sleek wall of cupboards and drawers, can be designed exactly to suit requirements, giving the right mix of hanging space, shelf space and drawer space.

Above A decorative feature has been made of the storage in this Shaker-style bedroom. Ranks of drawers have been fitted into a recess where you might expect to see cupboards. Dotted with the dark spots of their handles, they create a pleasing geometry, but remembering what is kept in each of them must be a daily challenge.

Left and far left Strikingly modern cupboards make a bold statement in the bedroom of this otherwise traditionally furnished period house. The deep doors contain extra storage and swing open to reveal hanging space and open drawers.

light, book, alarm clock and glass of water. Even a little corner shelf can save you having to fumble under the bed to find a tissue or turn off the beeping at 7am sharp. If there is room for only one other item of furniture, it should probably be a chair – not just for sitting on to do up your shoes or paint your toenails but as somewhere to drape a throw or put your clothes overnight.

If you still have empty floor space, you can add more furnishings, either useful pieces, such as a small desk, or primarily decorative ones, such as a pretty screen or indulgent chaise longue. Soft furnishings in a bedroom give it the feel of a boudoir – a haven to which you might retreat in the middle of the day, not only when you are ready for bed.

Above A modern interpretation of the Shaker fitted drawers on page 23, these square drawers are ideal for bulky jumpers and jeans.
Left Box shelving in a child's bedroom can be used for books, toys and games. Artfully arranged, it looks attractive, too.
Far left A bedside table with a cupboard and drawer is doubly useful. The extra storage means that you can afford to leave its top uncluttered.
Opposite A bedhead that is deep enough to be used as a shelf is a sleek alternative to a bedside table.

• **Parkinson's Law** applies to storage just as surely as to so many other aspects of life: however much you have, **you will surely fill it**.

• Don't forget the **dead space beneath the bed**. Some beds are designed to incorporate drawers; alternatively, boxes can hold a surprising amount concealed beneath **the overhang of a bedspread**.

• **Foldaway beds** used to require two strong men to raise and lower them. Modern versions are **elegant in looks** and operation and give you daytime **floor space** that would otherwise be unusable.

• A **full-length mirror** is essential not only for reasons of vanity; judiciously placed, it can also increase the **sense of space and light**.

window treatments
& soft furnishings

The softness and texture of fabrics are essential to the comfort of a bedroom. Just as the bed would be painfully unwelcoming without its sheets and blankets or duvet, an unadorned bedroom window can leave you feeling exposed and unsafe. Not that it is necessary to have acres of billowing fabric. Slatted shutters or blinds might suit your room better. But the style of window treatment you choose will not only be a question of looks; it will also depend on how much light you wish to exclude and how much privacy you need to gain.

Top These attractive sash windows might have been swamped by curtains. Instead, the owners have chosen blackout roller blinds, which disappear when not in use.
Above Thick woollen curtains provide a protective shield for a bed with its back to a window.
Right A bold gingham contrasted with airy white voile makes curtains that are both functional and pretty.
Opposite A wall of window in this sun-flooded room is veiled by sheer cotton. The folds of fabric filter the glare and soften the feel of the space.

Sometimes the only way to achieve the look you want, and make it practical, is to use a combination of fabrics, or fabrics and blinds.

White blackout blinds are an extremely effective means of cutting out light and can be used alone for a minimal look; tucked inside the window embrasure they barely show at all. However, for daytime privacy, you may want to add a layer of sheer curtain. If you would also like to minimize draughts and muffle noise, you can add yet another layer to your window treatment with heavy, lined curtains on top of the sheers – not quite as effective as double glazing, but possibly less expensive.

Once you have decided what you require in terms of function, you can enjoy playing with the aesthetics of your windows. Curtains, whether traditional chintz or crumpled linen, are the most feminine option and tend to make a room feel cosy and cut off from the outside world. Blinds, whether Roman, roller or Venetian, have a crisper, cooler look and take up less floor and wall space.

Like curtains, soft furnishings in a bedroom have a cocooning effect. If you have enough floor space for a squashy armchair, a chaise longue or even a sofa, this is a sure way to make your bedroom an irresistible haven at any time of the day. A chaise longue is particularly appropriate – a piece of furniture specially designed for lazy lounging, ideal for those times when you don't feel ready for bed but would rather recline than sit up.

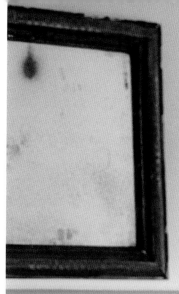

- Curtain material does not have to cost a fortune. **Unbleached linen scrim**, used by window cleaners, makes a stylish sheer, and old linen **sheets, lined or unlined**, look fresh and surprisingly modern.

- Make curtains unique with **a contrasting lining** or a wide band of fabric added to the leading edges or **along the bottom**. Aim for an interesting mix.

- Giving a more **architectural look** than curtains or blinds, well-fitting shutters provide good insulation against **light, noise and weather**.

- You may not have space for a sofa but you might be able to squeeze in **a small padded ottoman**, giving somewhere to sit and **extra storage** space.

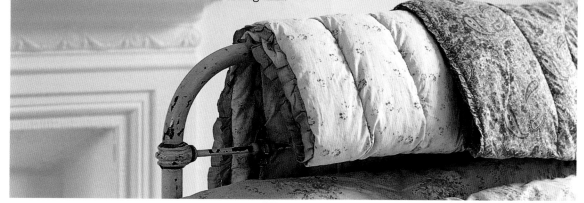

Above Vintage quilts add an extra layer of warmth to a bed, as well as the charm of faded florals.

Right Modern luxury takes the form of a silk-lined throw.

Opposite, above left A generous armchair with its companion stool is an invitation to sit with your feet up.

Opposite, above right Draped over the arm of a chair or the end of a bed, a downy throw represents the perfect accessory for bedroom lounging.

Opposite, below The chaise longue is a piece of furniture specifically designed for resting out of bed and makes an elegant addition to any bedroom.

lighting & display

As any film star will tell you, the difference between good and bad lighting is the difference between flattery and the unvarnished truth. Even the prettiest room is ruined by a harsh overhead light; better to have several ceiling spots, supplemented by table lamps. Bedroom lights should ideally be on a dimmer switch; otherwise, a choice of independent light sources allows you to control the illumination intensity. A strong light is desirable for checking your appearance in the mirror, but otherwise, in a room where you want to feel relaxed, softer lighting is more appropriate. Good directional reading lights are essential if you want to avoid eye strain.

Left A wall light beside the bed leaves more surface space to put things on; in this instance, there is room for a decorative glass bottle.
Far left The source of light from a bedside illumination should be above the reader's eye level, as in the case of this elegant table lamp.
Below Several different light sources allow maximum flexibility. The paper globe shade softens and diffuses the overhead lighting.
Opposite The simple lines and jaunty angle of a vintage lamp give it a strong presence in a modern bedroom. Its height and position just behind the reader are ideal for comfortable reading.

The right level of artificial light in a room can profoundly affect your comfort, as well as showing the room off at its most attractive.

While some types of light such as recessed spotlights are designed to be unobtrusive, other types can be decorative features in themselves. Obviously, function should take precedence over form – a stunning bedside lamp that gives out a faint green glow is a waste of space. However, given the huge choice of lighting now available, there is no reason why a light that does the job it is designed for should not also look good.

The only exception to the function-before-form rule applies to chandeliers, which may emit a light that is neither pleasing nor useful, but nonetheless make beautiful decorative mobiles hanging from the ceiling.

Closely linked with lighting is display, perhaps the most personal element of any room. As your bedroom is likely to be the space in the home that is least on show, you can please yourself with little decorative flourishes. This might be the place for your collection of handbags or glass candlesticks, for example. To avoid a cluttered look, group collections of things together. A wall of photographs, all in similar frames, looks less untidy than individual photographs scattered around the room propped on every available surface.

Top left A choice of lettering from old shop signs, arranged according to colour and font as opposed to sense, makes a quirky and amusing display on a bedroom wall.
Left A passion for red shoes is on show in this all-white bedroom with its specially designed shelves.

Above Deep suspended shelves in a child's bedroom make books the subject of an attractive display.
Right Where there is no space for a bedside table, as in this room, a wall light is the obvious solution, its switch conveniently positioned just above the pillow.

- Wall lights are **great space savers** and can be positioned above a bed at whatever height you find most **comfortable for reading**.

- The light from a table lamp is directed and coloured by its shade. A **pale parchment shade** gives a soft and diffused light.

- Bedrooms are private enough to allow a bit of decorative nostalgia, whether it is the moth-eaten rabbit you slept with as a child or your **favourite wedding photograph**.

- If you cannot afford curtains **in a fabric you love**, buy a single length of it and hang it from **a pole on the wall** behind your bed.

putting it

together

contemporary

Minimalism in its purest form is difficult for most people to live with. A less demanding version of the style achieves its effects with clean lines, plain surfaces and streamlined modern furnishings – for interiors with a calm, contemporary feel. If you want to create this look in a bedroom, it is essential to have ample and efficient storage.

Above Natural materials, such as the wood panelling behind this bed, play a vital part in humanizing the streamlined interior. Simple, sheer curtains filter the light and make a pleasing contrast with the smooth gloss of the wood.
Right The balance between areas of plain colour is well judged in this elegant room. The hugely enlarged photograph of a flower adds a striking dash of pattern and some organic curves.
Opposite The straight lines in this neat, stylish room are offset by textured fabrics. In addition to the deeply corded carpet, heavy bedspread and matching cushions, a slightly padded fabric has been used to panel the walls around the bed, making a cleverly integral bedhead.

The contemporary style is ideal for people who enjoy the discipline of perfect tidiness. A plain modern divan, dressed with crisp white bed linen, a simple bedside table and lamp, white walls, roller blinds – and there you have the essential ingredients of a contemporary-style bedroom. But the effect is easily ruined by, say, a clutter of shoes, discarded clothes or piles of magazines. Everything extraneous needs to be hidden away, ideally behind a wall of sleek cupboard doors.

However, as the pictures on these pages show, to make a room that is both simple and beautiful is a subtle and complicated business. Where you have only a few pieces, it is worth buying the best quality you can afford. The emptier and plainer a room, the more care needs to be taken over balance and contrast, whether between blocks of

Left This small bedroom, sectioned off from a larger room by a sliding door, has been pared down to the essentials. It gets its character from a sculptural armchair, a compelling piece of wall art and the sloping ceiling with hidden light source.

Above A clean, empty look is far easier to achieve when you have an expanse of floor space to play with. Sticking to a very limited palette of colours also helps. In this room, bright white has been used to contrast with natural wood.

colour, or shapes of furniture. For example, pairing a low bed with a tall cupboard can produce a dramatic effect. If the palette is limited to only a few colours, or to shades that are very similar to one another, then different textures are vital in order to provide visual, as well as tactile, variety.

Care must also be taken to ensure that a bedroom in the contemporary style does not feel too hard-edged. Where straight lines predominate, a curve or two will introduce variety of line, just as texture breaks the monotony of colour. Use natural materials such as glossy wood, heavy linen and soft cashmere to offset an impression of austerity. Often the plump mounds of pillows and the soft drape of a bedspread will be enough to counteract the effect of too many right angles.

plain colours, clean lines ...

When less is more, **quality matters**. Buy the best you can afford, particularly when choosing **bed linen and flooring**.

Very plain rooms can give an austere impression. **Use natural materials** to convey a feeling of luxury.

and no clutter

Be disciplined about tidiness and **make sure everything has a home**, from shoes and bags to boxes of paper tissues.

Use **balance and contrast** – for example, match a wall of dark wood with a wall of white curtain, a polished concrete floor with **a sheepskin rug**.

Right The exposed wooden framework of this country cottage has been augmented to make simple bunk beds. Clothes hang on pegs, as they did before the advent of the clothes hanger.

Below A floral quilt and a quaint antique lamp provide old-fashioned comfort and convenience.

Opposite New owners have left the interior walls of this 16th-century house almost untouched, with layers of limewash and scraps of wallpaper telling their own story about the history of its decoration. The antique furnishings also have a patina of age and look comfortably at home in their well-worn setting. Only the bed linen and ticking mattress are fresh and new.

country

Country style can be re-created anywhere from a cottage
in a field to the interior of a suburban semi. Its essence is
a relaxed, quiet nostalgia, and while beams, inglenooks and
uneven walls all add to the charm, they are not essential.
Above all, this is a style that allows for the shabby and the
quirky alongside simple, traditional furnishings and fabrics.

A country-style bed can be anything from a plain four-poster to a metal bedstead, as long as it is not too grand. An antique will have the patina acquired from years of wear and tear, but there are plenty of good reproduction versions to be found. Add an old-fashioned bedspread over the duvet, or rediscover the pleasures of sheets and blankets. Genuine antique quilts are expensive and often too fragile for daily use, but feather-filled eiderdowns from our grandmothers' era are easy to find in antique shops and market stalls, and make a pretty addition to any bed (shake them well before you buy just to make sure they are not losing too many feathers).

Since the country look is far from streamlined, it is worth considering freestanding as opposed to fitted storage. Old French armoires are particularly capacious, and antique chests-of-drawers – popular bedroom furnishings for more than 200 years – are plentiful. Good-quality chests-of-drawers are expensive, but you can always find something tatty and do it up yourself. In fact, expensive woods such as mahogany and rosewood don't tend to fit with the country look, which favours cheaper pine or painted furniture, preferably pieces

Left Panelling a room with painted match-boarding gives it instant country charm.
Below Cotton ticking, originally designed for use as mattress and pillow covers, is far too good to hide.
Bottom The contrast of textures between the slightly rough woollen blanket and the smooth cotton sheets make this bed look particularly inviting.
Opposite, above left The extra-large squares give this patchwork quilt a modern twist.
Opposite, below left and right Examples of recycling range from painted metal bedsteads from a school dormitory to a new bag made from old French table linen.

that are a bit chipped and rubbed. Wicker hampers and wooden chests make good storage for spare sheets and blankets or clothes that are out of season.

When looking for fabrics, choose traditional designs in cotton and linen; silks, velvets and damasks are too opulent for this homespun style. Ginghams, floral chintzes, floral sprigs and striped tickings all have the right look and feel. If you want to keep the effect really simple, stick to checks or stripes. For a more feminine look, mix in faded florals and monochrome toiles. A rose-scattered curtain trimmed with a border of checked gingham or a striped valance under a toile bedspread looks pretty as a picture.

Baskets are **light and strong** and make ideal storage for a country bedroom. Line **a wicker hamper** with cotton and it will also be dust-proof.

Unlined curtains look fresh and simple, and **waft in the breeze** when the window is open. To cut out light use discreet **blackout roller blinds**.

pretty, informal, welcoming . . . .

Fresh flowers, whether **cow parsley in a milk bottle** or garden roses in a glass jug, add beauty and **the scent of outdoors**.

Wooden floorboards and cotton rugs have **the right rustic feel**, or choose one of the natural mattings **such as coir or seagrass**.

a room for rest

classically elegant

Classical style, derived from Greek and Roman architecture, has been endlessly revived and reworked, adapted to suit 18th-century stately homes and 20th-century town halls. In its purest form it has been the preserve of the rich and powerful. But humbler, more accessible versions of classical style can also be seen in urban terraces and village houses.

Left The character of this room is defined by an imposing antique French bed, its dark wood and curvaceous carvings outlined against pure white walls. Barely-there curtains and the lack of any other decoration ensure that the bed is the unchallenged focus.

Below This painted chair with its cane seat and back is a copy of an 18th-century design.

Opposite A single piece of furniture can give a room a classical feel. In this bedroom, the piece is an unusual antique cupboard with arched doors flanked by pillars. The restrained colour scheme of white and lilac enhances the impression of refinement.

The classically elegant style is sophisticated and serene. Just as people who are tall and slim generally find it easier to dress elegantly, so it is a great advantage, if your chosen style is 'classical', to have rooms with high ceilings. Tall beds, long curtains, high cupboards – all are practical impossibilities unless you have at least two and a half vertical metres to play with. So this style is unlikely to be the best choice for a country cottage or an urban basement. However, many small city flats have been converted from houses that were once quite grand, and these spaces, with their typically tall windows, are well suited to classical elegance.

Height is important not only architecturally; a room furnished with a low divan, a low chest and nothing that reaches towards the ceiling lacks the necessary formality. A slim four-poster is ideal, perhaps draped with sheer, white cotton or left bare for a more austere look. Well-chosen antiques, whether a single chair or a set of architectural prints, will add to the understated glamour.

Fabrics can be opulent silks and velvets, if you can afford them, but you will achieve a more tranquil effect by keeping colours plain. Stripes in two colours have a strongly classical feel. Cheap cotton ticking, lined and made up into full-length curtains, can look surprisingly stately. If you want to introduce more pattern, choose a monochrome toile, but don't use too much of it or the room will start to take on a country feel.

Right Painted the colour of clotted cream, this French bedhead is as timelessly chic as a pale linen suit. **Far right** Antiques don't have to be opulent to be graceful, as this bentwood chair perfectly illustrates. **Below** The tall, tapered posts of the bed and its Shaker-style simplicity set the tone in a room that is both contemporary and classical. **Opposite, above left and right** Rooms furnished with antiques often have a soothing sense of permanence – one of the characteristics of the English country house style. **Opposite, below** The tall, slim, metal four-poster and the specially made cupboard in this bedroom are obviously modern, even though the design of both borrows ideas from antique furniture.

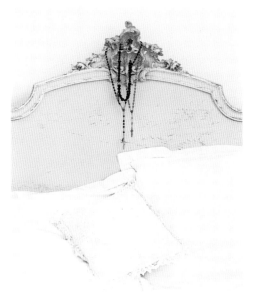

A large **mosquito net** makes an attractive and inexpensive bed canopy, adding **presence and height** to a simple divan.

A colour scheme made up of whites, off-whites and shades of cream is a **recipe for sophistication**.

cool, refined . . .

Make a ceiling look higher by painting walls with **wide vertical stripes** in different shades of the same colour.

Well-framed photocopies make a surprisingly **convincing substitute for antique prints**. Hang them in a group for maximum impact.

Give fitted cupboards panelled doors – it will make them look **more architectural**.

traditional and contemporary

small bedrooms

Smallness is usually seen as a disadvantage. But, carefully planned, a small bedroom can become an asset – the ultimate cosy hideaway where you can sleep feeling safe and secure, as snug as a bird in its nest. Bedroom necessities are few: a comfortable bed, a light to read by, a drawer or two, and some hanging space.

Above Older children love sleeping high above floor level, whether in a top bunk or, as here, on a specially made platform bed. Cupboards have been fitted into the space beneath the bed, leaving maximum floor area for play.

Left This bed has been built on a platform in a small but high-ceilinged space. The wide shelf next to the bed acts as bedside table, dressing table and book shelf, while the mirrored doors of the storage cupboards double the space visually and reflect light from the window opposite.

Opposite The steeply sloping ceiling of this attic bedroom has been panelled with plywood. The warm colour and naturally insulating properties of wood add to the feeling of cosiness and enclosure.

The most efficient way to use limited space is with fitted furniture. Most small bedrooms have at least one wall that can be fitted floor to ceiling with storage cupboards. In an old house, cupboards may fit best in the shallow recesses on either side of an original chimney breast. If you place your bed where the fireplace would once have been and continue the cupboards across the top to make an alcove for the bed, you gain even more cupboard space. In a room where wall space for storage is at a premium, consider placing the bed with its back to the window.

Beds can be built-in too, and designed to incorporate storage in that dead space underneath. A deep shelf as a bedhead makes a place to put a reading light, books and a glass of water, freeing up space that would otherwise be taken by bedside tables. Bunk beds are obvious space-savers for children's rooms. Some off-the-peg versions even incorporate desks and sofas underneath. Given sufficient ceiling height, a platform bed can be an equally good solution for adults. If the space beneath is used for cupboards, you have neatly provided two bedroom essentials in a single block.

Right A cosy bed, tucked in at the end of the room, is surrounded by storage. The high ceiling relieves any feeling of claustrophobia.

Below This compact sleeping space is separated from the rest of an apartment by sliding doors which are left open during the day.

Opposite, left When the sofa bed is folded away, this small, bright room converts into a sitting room and office space. The wall lights and the alcove of box shelving are appropriate to the changing functions of the room.

Opposite, right A spare bedroom has been created on a landing at the top of a steep ladder staircase. The bed folds out of a sleek, modern box and the open lid forms a bedhead.

When it comes to décor, there are two routes for a small room: one works to create the illusion of space; the other makes a virtue of necessity by emphasizing its inherently cosy, enclosing qualities. The first demands coherence, plain pale colours and a strict absence of clutter. A colour scheme of neutrals and naturals is soothing and not as demanding, or potentially dazzling first thing in the morning, as brilliant white.

Don't forget the power of mirrors – unrivalled for magnifying light and volume. Sliding mirrored doors can look sleek and modern while giving the illusion that a room is twice its size. Using mirrors to panel small areas of wall, alcoves and rebates can make even the most cramped space feel bright and airy.

If you are going for all-out cosiness, there is no better way to promote it than with fabric, whether with drapes of wafting muslin or the fat folds of heavy linen. It can even be used on the walls, stretched on battens like slightly textured wallpaper.

Sliding doors occupy **less space** than hinged doors. Use them for wardrobes and, if necessary, install **a sliding pocket door** into the room for extra wall space.

Thick full-length curtains use up precious floor space. Choose **Roman or roller blinds** instead.

small is beautiful . . .

small is cosy

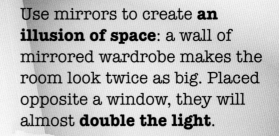

Use mirrors to create **an illusion of space**: a wall of mirrored wardrobe makes the room look twice as big. Placed opposite a window, they will almost **double the light**.

Your **mother was right**. Make the bed and put things away. Your room **will look bigger**.

suppliers

Amazing Emporium
249 Cricklewood Broadway
London NW2 6NX
020 8208 1616
www.amazingemporium.com
Beds including bateau lits,
daybeds and Art Deco styles.

And So To Bed
Showrooms nationwide
0808 1444343 for stockists
www.andsotobed.co.uk
Comprehensive range of
beds and bed linen.

B&Q
0845 3093099 for branches
www.diy.com
Paints and varnishes from
Benetton, Dulux and Crown.

Beaudesert
Old Imperial Laundry
London SW11 4XW
020 7720 4977
www.beaudesert.co.uk
Specialists in four-posters.

California Closets
Unit 8
Staples Corner Business Park
London NW2 7JP
020 8208 4544
www.calcosets.co.uk
Bespoke wardrobe systems.

Cath Kidston
8 Clarendon Cross
London W11 4AP
(and stockists)
020 7221 4000
www.cathkidston.co.uk
Retro floral fabrics and a
range of nostalgic bed linen.

Christopher Wray Lighting
8–10 Headingley Lane
Leeds LS6 2AS
0113 278 2653
www.christopherwray.com
020 7751 8701 for branches
Vast range of lighting.

The Conran Shop
Michelin House
81 Fulham Road
London SW3 6RD
020 7589 7401
www.conran.co.uk
Bedroom linens and furniture
in cutting-edge designs.

Couverture
310 Kings Road
London SW3 5UH
020 7795 1200
www.couverture.co.uk
Original and pretty designs for
bed linen; also mail order.

Designers Guild
267–271 Kings Road
London SW3 5EN
(and stockists)
020 7243 7300
www.designersguild.com
Fabrics and bed linen,
wallpaper and furniture.

Harriet Ann Sleigh Beds
Cherry Garden Farm
Hastings Road
Rolvenden, Cranbrook
Kent TN17 4PL
01580 243005 for brochure
and stockists
Wooden beds.

Heal's
196 Tottenham Court Road
London W1T 7LQ
020 7636 1666
www.heals.co.uk
Beds, bedroom furniture and
handmade mattresses.

The Holding Company
241–245 Kings Road
London SW3 5EL
020 7352 1600
(and mail order)
www.theholdingcompany.co.uk
Endless ideas for storage.

Ikea
0845 355 1141
www.ikea.co.uk
Budget bedroom furniture,
bed linen and ready-made
curtains.

Habitat
196 Tottenham Court Road
London W1T 9LD
020 7631 3880
0845 6010740 for branches
www.habitat.net
One-stop shopping for blinds,
beds, rugs, ready-made
curtains, bed linen, lighting
and storage.

The Iron Bed Company
83 Tottenham Court Road
London W1T 4SZ
020 7436 7707
01243 57888 for catalogue
www.ironbed.com
Nationwide showrooms and
huge mail order catalogue.

John Cullen Lighting
585 Kings Road
London SW6 2EH
020 7371 5400
www.johncullenlighting.co.uk
Extensive range of
contemporary light fittings
and a bespoke lighting
design service.

John Lewis
Oxford Street
London W1A 1EX
(and branches)
020 7629 7711
www.johnlewis.com
Fabrics and a wide range
of bed linens; also furniture
and lighting.

Junckers
01376 517512 for stockists
www.junckers.co.uk
Solid hardwood flooring.

Laura Ashley
0800 868 100
www.lauraashley.com
Chintzes and other traditional
designs; also reproduction
metal bedsteads and
bedroom furniture in natural
and painted wood. Stores
nationwide and mail order.

The London Wall Bed Company
430 Chiswick High Road
London W4 5TF
020 8742 8200
www.wallbed.co.uk
Pull-down beds.

McCloud Lighting
269 Wandsworth Bridge
Road
London SW6 2TX
020 7371 7151
www.mccloud.co.uk
Decorative metal lights, wall
lights and chandeliers, and
contemporary lighting.

Marks & Spencer
020 7268 1234 for branches
www.marksandspencer.com
Good-value modern classics.
On-line shopping available.

Melin Tregwynt
Tregwynt Mill
Castlemorris
Haverfordwest
Pembrokeshire SA62 5UX
01348 891225
www.melintregwynt.co.uk
Pure wool blankets and
throws in checks, plains and
pinstripes; also mail order.

Ocean
0870 2426283
www.Oceanuk.com
Modern furniture including
low, modern platform beds;
mail order only.

Peacock Blue
0870 333 1555
www.peacockblue.co.uk
Mail order bed linen. Perfect
for a country-style bedroom.

Oka
0870 160 6002
www.okadirect.com
Mail-order furniture, including
a painted range.

R J Norris
88 Coldharbour Lane
London SE5 9PU
020 7274 5306
www.norrisbedding.co.uk
Bespoke mattresses made
with natural fibres.

Roger Oates Design
The Long Barn
Eastnor
Ledbury
Herefordshire HR8 1EL
01531 631611 for stockists
www.rogeroates.com
Natural floorings.

Sanderson
01895 830044 for nationwide
stockists
www.sanderson-uk.com
Wallpaper, fabric and paint in
classic English style and a
range of bed linen to match.

Selfridges & Co.
08708 377 377
www.selfridges.co.uk
Department store with
branches in London,
Manchester and Birmingham.

The White Company
0870 900 9555
www.thewhiteco.com
Mail-order bed linen, throws
and accessories, including
cotton rib blankets, and
white-on-white embroidered
duvet covers and pillowcases.

credits

Key: ph=photographer, a=above, b=below, r=right, l=left, c=centre.

Front jacket Alan Williams/Katie Bassford King's house in London designed by Touch Interior Design

Page 1 ph Debi Treloar; **2** ph Chris Everard/a house in London designed by Helen Ellery of The Plot London; **3** ph Jan Baldwin/Gabriele Sanders' Long Island home; **4l** ph Jan Baldwin/Peter & Nicole Dawes' apartment, designed by Mullman Seidman Architects; **4c** ph Jan Baldwin/Olivia Douglas & David DiDomenico's apartment in New York, designed by CR Studio Architects, PC; **4r** ph Debi Treloar/new build house in Notting Hill designed by Seth Stein Architects; **5** ph Chris Tubbs/Nickerson–Wakefield House in upstate New York/anderson architects; **6–7** ph Debi Treloar/family home, Bankside, London; **8l** ph Debi Treloar/Elizabeth Alford & Michael Young's loft in New York; **8c** ph Debi Treloar/Sarah Munro and Brian Ayling's home in London; **8–9** ph Chris Everard/Bob & Maureen Macris' apartment on Fifth Avenue in New York designed by Sage Wimer Coombe Architects; **9r** ph Chris Everard/an apartment in London designed by Jo Hagan of Use Architects; **10** ph Jan Baldwin/interior designer Didier Gomez's apartment in Paris; **11a** ph Debi Treloar/Ben Johns & Deb Waterman Johns' house in Georgetown; **11b** ph Chris Tubbs/Vermont Shack/Ross Anderson, anderson architects; **12** ph Debi Treloar/Ian Hogarth's family home; **12–13** ph Alan Williams/Richard Oyarzarbal's apartment in London designed by Urban Research Laboratory; 13r Alan Williams/Selworthy apartment in London designed by Gordana Mandic & Peter Tyler at Buildburo (www.buildburo.co.uk); **14bl** ph Alan Williams/owner of Gloss, Pascale Bredillet's own apartment in London; **14ar** ph Alan Williams/Donata Sartorio's apartment in Milan; **14br** ph Andrew Wood/an apartment in London designed by Littman Goddard Hogarth; **15l** ph Jan Baldwin/a house in New York designed by Brendan Coburn and Joseph Smith from Coburn Architecture; **15r** ph Polly Wreford/Louise Jackson's house in London; **16l** ph Tom Leighton; **16ar** ph James Merrell/Janie Jackson, stylist/designer; **16br & 17** ph Alan Williams/Katie Bassford King's house in London designed by Touch Interior Design; **18l** ph Chris Everard/Jo Warman – Interior Concepts; **18–19** ph Jan Baldwin/Emma Wilson's house in London; **19** ph Chris Everard/apartment in New York designed by Gabellini Associates; **20l** ph Andrew Wood/Johanne Riss' house in Brussels; **20ar** ph Catherine Gratwicke/Claudia Bryant's house in London-headboard designed by Claudia Bryant; **20–21b** ph Chris Everard/an apartment in New York designed by Steven Learner; **21a** both Tom Leighton; **21c** ph Jan Baldwin; **21b** ph Jan Baldwin/Peter & Nicole Dawes' apartment, designed by Mullman Seidman Architects; **22al** ph Andrew Wood/media executive's house in Los Angeles, architect: Stephen Slan, builder: Ken Duran, furnishings: Russell Simpson, original architect: Carl Maston c.1945; **22ar** ph Jan Baldwin/Emma Wilson's house in London; **22b** ph Debi Treloar; **23a** ph Simon Upton; **23b** both ph Chris Everard/François Muracciole's apartment in

Paris; **24a&bl** ph Chris Everard/Mark Weinstein's apartment in New York designed by Lloyd Schwan; **24br** ph Debi Treloar/Sarah Munro and Brian Ayling's home in London; **25** ph Debi Treloar/family home, Bankside, London; **26** ph Ray Main/ Robert Callender & Elizabeth Ogilvie's studio in Fife designed by John C Hope Architects; **27al** ph Jan Baldwin/Olivia Douglas & David DiDomenico's apartment in New York, designed by CR Studio Architects, PC; **27bl** ph Jan Baldwin/designer Chester Jones' house in London; **27r** ph Catherine Gratwicke/designer Caroline Zoob's home in East Sussex; **28al** ph Chris Everard/Central Park West Residence, New York City designed by Bruce Bierman Design, Inc.; **28ar&b** ph Tom Leighton; **29a** Catherine Gratwicke; **29b** ph Tom Leighton; **30** ph Chris Everard/apartment of Amy Harte Hossfeld and Martin Hossfeld; **31al** ph Ray Main/Jonathan Reed's apartment in London, light from William Yeoward; **31ar** ph Jan Baldwin/Gabriele Sanders' Long Island home; **31b** ph Chris Everard/Jo Warman – Interior Concepts; **32a&bl** ph Catherine Gratwicke/Laura Stoddart's apartment in London; **32r** ph Debi Treloar; **33 ph** Ray Main/a loft in London designed by Nico Rensch, light from SKK; **34–35** ph Chris Everard/Mark Weinstein's apartment in New York designed by Lloyd Schwan; **36** ph Chris Everard/an actor's London home designed by Site Specific; **36–37** ph Andrew Wood/Roger and Suzy Black's apartment in London designed by Johnson Naylor; **37r** ph Chris Everard/Eric De Queker's apartment in Antwerp; **38l** ph Debi Treloar/new build house in Notting Hill designed by Seth Stein Architects; **38r** ph Andrew Wood/Johanne Riss' house in Brussels; **39a** both ph Alan Williams/Alannah Weston's house in London designed by Stickland Coombe Architecture; **39b** ph Jan Baldwin/art dealer Gul Coskun's apartment in London; **40al** ph Jan Baldwin/designer Chester Jones' house in London; **40cl** ph Chris Everard/Jo Warman – Interior Concepts; **40bl** ph Andrew Wood/media executive's house in Los Angeles, architect: Stephen Slan, builder: Ken Duran, furnishings: Russell Simpson, original architect: Carl Maston c.1945; **40r** ph Alan Williams/the architect Voon Wong's own apartment in London; **41al** ph Jan Baldwin/Gabriele Sanders' Long Island home; **41bl** ph Chris Everard/the London apartment of the Sheppard Day Design Partnership; 41ar ph Andrew Wood/ Richard and Sue Hare's house in Idaho designed by Mark Pynn A.I.A. of McMillen Pynn Architecture L.L.P.; **42l** ph Chris Tubbs/Daniel Jasiak's home near Biarritz; **42r** ph Christopher Drake/Melanie Thornton's house in Gloucestershire; **43** ph Tom Leighton; **44al** ph Catherine Gratwicke/Rose Hammick's home in London–French antique sheet awning form Kim Sully Antiques, patchwork quilt by Emily Medley, shawl and flip-flops cushion from Grace & Favour, bed from Litvinof & Fawcett; **44bl** ph Tom Leighton; **44r** ph Catherine Gratwicke; **45l** ph Chris Tubbs/Mike and Deborah Geary's beach house in Dorset; **45ar** ph Tom Leighton; **45br** ph Tom Leighton/Mr Hone's 17th-century hutt in Shropshire; **46al** ph Debi Treloar; **46bl** ph Catherine Gratwicke; **46r** ph Simon Upton; **47a** ph Chris Tubbs/Daniel Jasiak's home near Biarritz; **47bl** ph Jan Baldwin/Gabriele Sanders' Long Island home; **47br** ph Chris Tubbs/Vermont Shack/Ross Anderson, anderson architects; **48** ph

Chris Everard/the London apartment of the Sheppard Day Design Partnership; **48–49** ph Alan Williams/Katie Bassford King's house in London designed by Touch Interior Design; **49** ph Jan Baldwin/art dealer Gul Coskun's apartment in London; **50a** both ph Alan Williams/Miv Watts' house in Norfolk; **50b** ph Chris Everard/Lisa & Richard Frisch's apartment in New York designed by Patricia Seidman of Mullman Seidman Architects; **51al** ph Catherine Gratwicke/Martin Barrell & Amanda Sellers' flat, owners of Maisonette, London; **51ar** ph Tom Leighton; **51b** ph Alan Williams/Stanley & Nancy Grossman's apartment in New York designed by Jennifer Post Design; **52ar** ph Jan Baldwin/interior designer Didier Gomez's apartment in Paris; **52c** ph Chris Everard/an apartment in Paris, designed by architect Paul Collier; **52bl** ph Tom Leighton/Roger & Fay Oates' house in Herefordshire; **53l&ar** ph Andrew Wood/Johanne Riss' house in Brussels; **53br** ph Tom Leighton/Roger & Fay Oates' house in Herefordshire; **54** ph Chris Tubbs/ Nickerson–Wakefield House in upstate New York/anderson architects; **55l** ph Chris Everard/an apartment in Milan designed by Tito Canella of Canella & Achilli Architects; **55ar** ph Debi Treloar/Julia & David O'Driscoll's house in London; **56al** ph Chris Everard/an apartment in New York, designed by Mullman Seidman Architects; **56ar** ph Chris Everard/a London apartment designed by architect Gavin Jackson; **56–57** ph Chris Everard/Pemper and Rabiner home in New York, designed by David Khouri of Comma; **57a** ph Chris Tubbs/Vermont Shack/Ross Anderson, anderson architects; **58al** ph Chris Everard/an actor's London home designed by Site Specific; **58bl** ph Debi Treloar/Sophie Eadie's house in London; **58r** ph Chris Everard/Adèle Lakhdari's home in Milan; **59l** ph Chris Everard/a house in London designed by Helen Ellery of The Plot London; **59ar** ph Debi Treloar/Kristiina Ratia and Jeff Gocke's family home in Norwalk, Connecticut; **59br** both ph Chris Everard/architect Jonathan Clark's home in London.

Architects and designers whose work is featured in this book

27.12 Design Ltd.
+1 212 727 8169
www.2712design.com
Page 30.

Elizabeth Alford Design
+1 212 385 2185
esa799@banet.net
Page 8l.

anderson architects
+1 212 620 0996
www.andersonarch.com
Pages 5, 11b, 47br, 54, 57a.

Brian Ayling, Artist
020 8802 9853
Pages 8c, 24br.

Joanne Barwick
P.O. Box 982
Boca Grande
Florida 33921
USA
Page 46r.

Bruce Bierman Design, Inc.
+1 212 243 1935
www.biermandesign.com
Page 28al.

Claudia Bryant
020 7602 2852
Page 20ar.

buildburo ltd
020 7352 1092
www.buildburo.co.uk
Page 13r.

Canella & Achilli Architects
+39 024695222
www.canella-achilli.com
Pages 55l, 58r.

Jonathan Clark Architects
020 7286 5676
jonathan@jonathanclarkarchitects.
co.uk
Page 59br both.

Coburn Architecture
+1 718 875 5052
www.coburnarch.com
Page 15l.

Paul Collier
+33 1 53 72 49 32
paul.collier@architecte.net
Page 52c.

David Khouri
Comma
+1 212 420 7866
www.comma-nyc.com
Pages 56–57.

Coskun Fine Art London
020 7581 9056
www.coskunfineart.com
Pages 39b, 49.

CR Studio Architects, PC
+1 212 989 8187
www.crstudio.com
Pages 4c, 27al.

Dive Architects
020 7407 0955
www.divearchitects.com
Pages 6–7, 25.

Eric De Queker
DQ – Design In Motion
Koninklijkelaan 44
2600 Bercham
Belgium
Page 37r.

Gabellini Associates
+1 212 388 1700
Page 19.

Gloss Ltd
020 8960 4146
pascale@glossltd.u-net.com
Page 14bl.

John C Hope Architects
0131 315 2215
Page 26.

Interior Concepts
020 8508 9952
www.jointeriorconcepts.co.uk
Pages 18l, 31b, 40cl.

Gavin Jackson
07050 097561
Page 56ar.

Janie Jackson/Palma Lilac
020 8960 9239
Page 16ar.

Jackson's
020 7792 8336
Page 15r.

Daniel Jasiak
+33 1 45 49 13 56
Pages 42l, 47a.

Johnson Naylor
020 7490 8885
brian.johnson@johnsonnaylor.co.uk
Pages 36–37.

Chester Jones Ltd
020 7498 2717
chester.jones@virgin.net
Pages 27bl, 40al.

Steven Learner Studio
+1 212 741 8583
www.stevenlearnerstudio.com
Pages 20–21b.

Littman Goddard Hogarth
020 7351 7871
www.lgh-architects.co.uk
Pages 12, 14br.

Maisonette
020 8964 8444
maisonetteUK@aol.com
Page 51al.

McMillen Pynn Architecture L.L.P.
+1 208 622 4656
www.sunvalleyachitect.com
Page 41ar.

Emily Medley
emilymedley@mac.com
Page 44al.

Mullman Seidman Architects
+1 212 431 0770
www.mullmanseidman.com
Pages 4l, 21b, 50b, 56al.

François Muracciole
+33 1 43 71 33 03
francois.muracciole@libertysurf.fr
Pages 23b both.

Roger Oates Design
Rugs and Runners Mail Order
Catalogue:
01531 631611
www.rogeroates.co.uk
Pages 52bl, 53br.

OryGomez
+33 01 44 30 8823
email: orygomez@free.fr
Pages 10, 52ar.

Helen Ellery
The Plot London
020 7251 8116
www.theplotlondon.com
Pages 2, 59l.

Jennifer Post Design
+1 212 734 7994
jpostdesign@aol.com
Page 51b.

Kristiina Ratia Designs
+1 203 852 0027
Page 59ar.

Reed Creative Services Ltd
020 7565 0066
Page 31al.

Nico Rensch
www.architeam.co.uk
Page 33.

Johanne Riss
+32 2 513 0900
Pages 20l, 38r, 53l, 53ar.

Sage Wimer Coombe Architects
+1 212 226 9600
Pages 8–9.

Lloyd Schwan/Design
+1 212 375 0858
lloydschwan@earthlink.net
Pages 24a & bl, 34–35.

Sheppard Day Design Partnership
020 7821 2002
Pages 41bl, 48.

Site Specific Ltd
020 7490 3176
www.sitespecificltd.co.uk
Pages 36, 58al.

Stephen Slan A.I.A.
+1 323 467 4455
Pages 22al, 40bl.

Seth Stein Architects
020 8968 8581
www.sethstein.com
Pages 4r, 38l.

Stickland Coombe Architecture
020 7924 1699
nick@scadesign.freserve.co.uk
Page 39a both.

Touch Interior Design
020 7498 6409
Pages 16br, 17, 48–49.

Urban Research Lab
020 8709 9060
www.urbanresearchlab.com
Pages 12–13.

USE Architects
020 8986 8111
use.arch@virgin.net
Page 9r.

Miv Watts at House Bait
01328 730557
miv.watts@virgin.net
Page 50a both.

Emma Wilson
www.45crossleyst.com
Pages 18–19, 22ar.

Voon Wong Architects
020 7587 0116
voon@btconnect.com
Page 40r.

Caroline Zoob
Commissions 01273 479274
Caroline Zoob's work is also
available at:
Housepoints 020 7978 6445
Page 27r.

index